A Titanic Hero: Thomas Byles

by Cady Crosby

Chapter 1

It was February 26, 1870. Just five years after the American Civil War came to a close and the same year that British author Charles Dickens died, **Roussel Davids Byles** was born in Staffordshire, England.

His father, the Reverend Alfred Byles, had recently been named pastor of the new Congregational Church at Headingley Hill.

With his serious brown eyes and over-large head, Roussel was not the most beautiful child. When the proud parents brought their little son to church, all the women in town whispered and said that he looked more like a college professor than a new baby. But Alfred and Louisa Byles were proud of their newborn son.

Within a few years, Reverend and Mrs. Byles moved their growing family to a bigger house in Yorkshire, England. By now, Roussel was big brother to six siblings. He loved to play with his three brothers, William, Winter and Lawrence. And when his three sisters, Mary, Hilda, and Helen, were born, Roussel welcomed them joyfully.

The Byles Family. Roussel is on the far left.
Circa 1880

Roussel loved school; and being the serious boy that he was, studied hard and tried to be the best student that he could be. Soon, Roussel found that he was particularly good at math. He enjoyed solving equations, he liked multiplying and dividing; he relished everything about math!

As a matter of fact, Roussel was so good at math that his teacher asked him to tutor some of the younger children who were having trouble. Roussel worked diligently at this new task. He had a gift for teaching that he readily shared with others. The village mothers laughed, and said that the serious baby had really become a little professor!

Roussel especially enjoyed spending time with one little boy whose name was Eddy. Eddy had a very hard time memorizing the multiplication facts. "I can't do it, Roussel! I don't understand why math is so important!"

"That's okay, Eddy. It is good to practice doing things that are hard. You want strong muscles don't you?"

"Well, of course I do! Why do you think I'm on the football team? But what do muscles have to do with math?" Eddy asked, looking even more confused.

"I wasn't talking about physical muscles, even though those are important too. Doing hard things builds our *character* muscles, Eddy. Just three more problems and you'll finish working out your character muscles; then you can go outside and play football."

After school, Roussel came home and did his homework or read his favorite literature. Reading suited both his studious nature and his frail body, for Roussel's health had never been the best. But reading was the one thing he loved that did not physically tax him.

One day, after Roussel finished his homework and was reading, Lawrence came in the room. "Roussel, will you please come play with me?" he asked.

Professional photograph of Lawrence Byles

"No," Roussel replied, not looking up. "Can't you see that I'm reading, Lawrence?"

Lawrence's face fell. "You're *always* reading, Roussel! Don't you ever have time to play with me? I never get to see you anymore."

Roussel began to respond, but saw his mother come in the room and shake her head at him, so he kept quiet.

Lawrence continued, "You're at school all day, then when you come home, you stay in your room until dinner. Then after dinner you read. You play with your books more than you play with me."

The back of Lawrence Byles' photograph. In the late 1800's, photographs were rare and expensive. These pictures would have been prized possessions in the Byles household.

Coming to sit by the boys, Mrs. Byles put her arms around her frustrated sons. "Roussel, I agree with Lawrence. You know that I love what a good student you are, and that I place a high importance on education. But what do you think is the better choice: to keep doing what *you* want, or to give your brother what he needs? Sometimes it is better to sacrifice what we want to do in order to make time for things that others need from us. Lawrence needs to see that you love him, and that you are willing to show that love by spending time with him."

"But Mother, you know how hard it is for me to run or do anything like that."

"Roussel," his mother continued. "You and I both know that even though you might not be able to do *everything*, you can certainly do *something* with your younger brother.

Give what you have."

The logic of his mother's words made sense. "Yes, Mother," Roussel said as he closed his book and stood up. "What do you want to play, Lawrence?"

"Oh, thank you, Roussel! Can you please come cycling with me? Father just replaced the spokes on the front wheel."

Looking a bit longingly at the book he was leaving behind, Roussel took heart when he saw the joy that radiated from Lawrence's face and ran to catch up with Lawrence.

Louisa, Mary, and Helen Byles

Chapter 2

Sunday mornings were always busy in the Byles' household. Rev. Byles rushed to get his papers in order for his sermon, and Mrs. Byles busied herself preparing their lunch early so it would be almost ready when they returned. One particular morning, Mrs. Byles called to her oldest son, "Roussel! Will you please put on Helen's shoes?"

Roussel looked up from where he was studying his Sunday school verses. "Yes, Mother. Come on Helen, I'll help you get ready for church."

Little Helen stamped her foot and scowled at her oldest brother. "I don't want to go to church! It's too long!"

"Not if you have a sweet," whispered Roussel, smiling at Helen and slipping a piece of toffee into her small hand. Tying off the last knot, Roussel stood up and took Helen's hand. "Now we're ready to go."

As the Byles family rode towards the Congregational Church, Rev. Byles told his wife, "I hope to encourage everyone to give generously to the funds drive this weekend. The poor need our assistance more than ever."

Roussel looked up from his book. "You mean like *Oliver*

Twist, Father? Charles Dickens talks a lot about the poor in that book."

Before their father could respond, Helen pulled on Roussel's jacket. "I want to give to the funds drive too!"

Reaching into his pocket, Roussel pulled out a copper and handed it to his sister. "Here, you can give this. But be sure not to lose it."

When they arrived at church, the family took their place in the front pew. After the first hymn, the Reverend Byles began his sermon.

"Brothers and sisters, today's verse is taken from Matthew 25:40:

> *'And the King shall answer and say unto them,*
> *Verily I say unto you, Inasmuch as ye have done it*
> *unto one of the least of these my brethren, ye have*
> *done it unto me.'*

Today, the funds drive that began two weeks ago is drawing to a close, and I call on each of you to *give what you have* to these, the least of our brethren. All proceeds from this funds drive go to clothing, feeding, and caring for the sick and poor, not only here in Shelton-Hanley, but in other parts of England as well."

As he listened to his father's sermon, Roussel fingered the precious shillings that he had in his pocket and his mind wandered. Just one more day, and he could purchase the Charles Dickens novel, *Great Expectations,* that he had been wanting for months. But as he listened to what his father was saying, Roussel began to think more about where his hard-earned money should go.

"Now, if for any reason your financial position is not such that you can give money, your contribution is still valuable. *Give what you have.* Whether that is your prayers, money, or support, we would be more than appreciative."

English shillings.
This is similar to the currency that Roussel Byles would have used. Circa 1880's.

Roussel thought about that last statement of his father's. *Give what you have.* He looked over at his mother, and she smiled at him. Roussel knew that she too was thinking of their conversation about Lawrence.

As he saw everyone around him pulling out their banknotes, he lightly touched the coins in his pocket. Could God be calling him, a 12 year old, to give up his book and give to the poor instead? Were the "least of His brethren" Roussel's brothers too?

Summoning all the self-control he could muster, Roussel stood with Helen and when she put her small copper into the basket, he placed his shillings in as well.

Chapter 3

Roussel's love of learning was not yet satisfied by the time he completed his general education at the age of sixteen.

He wanted to learn even more about math, history, and also about religion.

When he attended Rossall School, Roussel had quickly learned that he had a

Interior of Rossall School Chapel.

particular affinity for these three subjects. He had loved Rossall School, and wanted to continue studying for as long as he could.

Roussel Byles (far left) at Rossall School.

Rev. and Mrs. Byles agreed that Roussel should have the best education possible, so they sent him to Balliol College at the University of Oxford. To his delight, Roussel discovered that the college sponsored a debating society, and because he loved a good discussion with differing opinions, Roussel eagerly became a member.

Because Roussel was studying religion at Balliol, his vista

of knowledge grew wider. He learned more about both his religion and others. He learned about the English Reformation that took place in the 1500's, and Roussel researched more than was required of him to find out about this event.

Roussel's study brought him to question whether or not the faith that he grew up with was really true. When he came home from school on Christmas vacation, he got a chance to discuss this query with his brother William.
"I'm having doubts, Will. I've been reading some things at Balliol that have made me look closer at the Congregationalist church and whether or not it is truly one, holy, catholic, and apostolic. It doesn't seem to have all four of those marks. To be quite honest, the church that

King Henry VIII ultimately split from in 1534, the Roman Catholic Church, seems to fit those four marks perfectly."

William grinned at his older brother. "Well, everyone knows that if you have doubts about anything, you're guaranteed to do more than your fair share of research!" William's brow furrowed as he continued to speak. "But I agree with you, Roussel. I've been discovering things that lead me toward Rome too."

"Then what do you say to writing each other and discussing this?" Roussel asked.

"You know I'd be willing to do that. But let me tell you one thing, Roussel. Mother and Father will not understand this."

The two brothers looked at each other with dismay. Roussel was the first to speak. "Yes William, I know. However, doubt is not something to be trifled with. Doubt is just a step along the path-it's not an end. There must be a resolution. Remember the question Pontius Pilate asked? "What is truth?" I believe we must all seek the truth- no matter where it takes us. I feel like God is calling me, and I know that I have to follow."

Chapter 4

In the ensuing months, William and Roussel carried on a lengthy correspondence about their spiritual journey. Both men studied the Scriptures, creeds, and researched intensely. Eventually, William and Roussel both reached the same conclusion: that the answers to all their questions rested in the Catholic Church. After much prayer and self-reflection, Roussel was

Saint Thomas Aquinas

received into the Church on the Feast of Corpus Christi, 1894.

As he stood before the bishop at Confirmation and was asked what name he would take, Roussel replied, "Thomas."

One of Father Byles' patrons, the Doubting Apostle St. Thomas.

When the bishop's hands came to rest on Roussel's head, he could feel the sustaining presence of two mighty spiritual companions—the Patron Saint of Scholars, Thomas Aquinas, and the (doubting) Apostle Thomas. Surely the prayers of his patrons had accompanied him along the path that brought him to this day.

As life went on, Roussel (now Thomas Roussel Byles) felt called yet again. He had learned that when God is calling, his job was to be still and listen. God spoke to the quiet of his soul and Thomas heard God calling him—inviting him—to become one of His priests.

"Me, Lord? I've only just become Catholic. I'm not in the best of health. There are so many others. Why would you pick me?"

But as Thomas began to doubt his call, he was reminded of the story of Moses. Moses protested, "Lord! I cannot speak. Pick someone who can speak to your people." But the Lord said, "No. It is you I want."

The Church of St. Apollinaris today.

Thus, with confidence and humility, Thomas submitted his will and his wants to God, and began his studies to become a Catholic priest. Because almost his whole life had been devoted to study, the challenges of the seminary were small for Thomas. He studied in Rome and was ordained at the Church of Saint Apollinaris on June 15, 1902.

Chapter 5

After staying in Rome for three more years, Father Thomas Byles was assigned to a parish in Essex, England, in 1905. The parish was called St. Helen's and was a small church in the middle of a much larger country mission.

St. Helen's Catholic Church.

Soon after arriving at St. Helen's, Father Byles made the acquaintance of a nearby pastor, Father Edward Watson. The two became fast friends and traveled together to serve their parishes.

One evening as they were sitting and talking, Father Watson mentioned, "Thomas, I meant to tell you. I'm afraid I won't be able to come over next week as we had planned. I'll be cycling out to a neighboring mission to say Mass."

Father Byles' eyes lit up. "Would it disturb you much if I come with you? I would love to come and learn more about our people."

Father Watson raised his eyebrows. "My good man, may I remind you that you are not in the best of health? Cycling is a strictly physical exercise, and with your limp, it may harm you. You are a scholar and Balliol graduate, not a cyclist."

But Father Byles was already pulling out and dusting off, and he shrugged off Father Watson's protests with a smile.

The following Thursday, the two priests set off on their bicycles. As Father Watson watched in amazement, Father Byles confidently pedaled down the path, and as he rapidly outpaced Father Watson, called over his shoulder, "Come along, Edward! Our sheep are waiting for us!"

> *"When I first made his acquaintance and he proposed to go with me on the bicycle, I opened my eyes; he would have to go a considerable pace, I understand he was an invalid. Yes, but not in the matter of bicycling. So I found to my cost, especially going up-hill, and I shall not forget the effort it wrung from me to keep the lead on a certain evening late in last September, or how, I was urged to greater flight and fright by the sight I saw over my shoulder, as of some preternatural jockey, bending to his work, dogging every revolution of my wheels."*
> -Monsignor Edward Watson

Father Watson and Father Byles continued to visit on a weekly basis, and in 1908, Father Byles learned about a new youth movement that had recently gained popularity in England.

"Watson!" Father Byles called, knocking on his friend's door one sunny January morning.

Father Watson opened the door and grinned at his friend. "Come in, come in. I've just put a pot of tea on. We can have a nice chat."

Father Byles entered the room, but he was so excited that he couldn't even sit. "Edward, I've just learned about something marvelous that could really change the face of St. Helen's. A fellow by the name of Lord Baden-Powell has invented what he calls "the noble game of Scouting." Here's the manual that they've just published. I think that

Lord Robert Baden-Powell, founder of Boy Scouts.

the boys of the parish could really benefit from this."

Leaning over and taking the book from Father Byles' hands, Father Watson paged through the manual. "You're right, it does sound very beneficial. But again Father, think of your health! I don't see how you can add camping, hiking, and swimming to your already busy schedule. If you overtax yourself, you might end up in a hospital."

Father Byles' eyes sparkled with excitement. "How hard can it be, Father? These boys need a St. Helen's Boy Scout troop."

Chapter 6

"Father, Father!"

Father Byles finished lighting the stove under his tea pot and hurried to the front door where he greeted Tommy with a smile. "Why, hello Tommy! How are you this afternoon?"

"I'm well, Father," Tommy answered and removed his hat as he entered the small house. "I have a question for you about Boy Scouts. Do you have a moment?"

"Of course. What do you need?"

Two Boy Scouts practicing boxing, circa. 1910.

"Well, Father Byles, the boys and I are working on the Master at Arms merit badge right now, and we've already finished the fencing requirement. We have chosen boxing as the second requirement, and we were wondering if you could teach us."

Father Byles chuckled nervously and thought to himself, "*Me*, teach boxing?" But to Tommy he said kindly, "I'll consider it. I'll let you know tomorrow after morning Mass. You will serve at the altar for me tomorrow, won't you?"

"Of course, Father."

As Father Byles shut the door, his brow furrowed. He sighed, and whispered, "Domine, in auxilium meum!" *(Help me, Lord!")*

A few minutes later, and as though in answer to prayer, a childhood memory came to him and a smile lit up his face. He could almost hear his mother saying, "*Give what you have, Roussel.*"

A professional picture of Father Thomas Byles.

Thinking out loud, Father Byles murmured to himself, "I may not be good at boxing, but I *am* good at studying. I could get a book on boxing, and read it. If I stayed just one step ahead of the boys, this could work!"

The thought grew in his imagination. Walking over to his plentifully stacked bookshelves, Father Byles began searching diligently for any information on boxing, until the high-pitched whistle of the teapot interrupted his musings.

Chapter 7

After serving Mass the following morning, Tommy spoke to Father Byles as both were taking off their liturgical robes.

"Father, were you able to make a decision about boxing yesterday?"

"As a matter of fact, I have," Father Byles responded. "I've decided that I will try to teach you boxing. But it will have to be after all schoolwork is completed, and you must never, ever, use what I have taught you to purposely hurt another fellow."

"Of course, Father," Tommy cried excitedly.

"We should be able to work on boxing every week. If you really want to learn, we have to practice. But I won't be available during the month of April, because I have prior commitments.

"You see, my brother William just told me that he is getting married in April. He would like

> "In 1905 Father Thomas Byles, a diocesan missionary priest was appointed. He was a learned man and a good preacher and a caring pastor to his people. Some Ongar boys, wanting to learn to box, had reason to remember him for the rest of their lives. He took on their instruction, using a large shed behind the church."
> ~Ongar Millennium History Society

me to officiate the wedding, so I'll have to leave sometime during the week after Easter."

"But Father, last week when I asked you about your family, you said William might become a priest. Then you weren't able to tell us the rest of the story. Why didn't your brother end up becoming a priest?" Tommy asked, leaning against the counter.

"William was searching and praying for a very long time, Tommy," said Father Byles. "However, he ended up realizing that his vocation was not to become a priest. William then moved to New York to start a rubber business. And I found out last week that he is getting married to Miss Katherine Russell. Do you mind talking while we walk, Tommy?"

"Of course, Father. What ship is taking you?" questioned Tommy as the two walked outside.

"I'll be leaving on a White Star liner. William is paying for my ticket," replied Father Byles.

The White Star Line was a prominent shipping company.

Tommy gasped. The White Star line was known for its luxurious ships and was especially well-known because of their newest ship, the *Titanic*. She was the biggest ocean

WHITE STAR LINE.

OLYMPIC. 45000 TONS

TITANIC. 45000 TONS

THE LARGEST STEAMERS IN THE WORLD.

STEAMERS BUILT IN IRELAND.

QUEENSTOWN-NEW YORK
ON THURSDAYS AND FRIDAYS

QUEENSTOWN-BOSTON
ON WEDNESDAYS

JOHN DENNEHY,
Insurance Agent, CAHIRCIVEEN, &c. &c.

Late 1911 advertisement for the RMS *Titanic*.

liner that had ever been built.

"Father, isn't that the line that built the *Titanic*?" the young boy asked.

"Yes Tommy, it is. But I'm not going on the *Titanic*. It would be much too fancy and expensive for me," Father Byles replied.

"I've heard that not even God could sink the *Titanic*," Tommy murmured, half to himself.

Hearing this, Fr. Byles told Tommy firmly, "Never believe something like that. We are all in God's hands Tommy. Now, you should be off to school-I wouldn't want you to be late! And I need to write a letter to my brother."

Waving good-bye to Tommy, Father Byles strolled the remaining distance to his rectory. Once inside, he walked over to his oak desk, a graduation present from his parents. After he pulled out his pen and paper, Father Byles penned a letter to William.

The designation RMS stands for Royal Mail Steamer. The RMS *Titanic* was contracted to carry the British Royal Mail

My Dear W.

I am not at all sure that the English form of marriage is the same as is used in America. If not it might be better to get what you want in America. Is her name Isabella Katherine? I want to have this accurate. Of course the difference between the English would only be slight – the words in England are the clauses beginning, "I N., take thee N. to my wedded (wife/husband)—

Perhaps it is worth mentioning to you that the Cardinal has notified his intention of celebrating his elevation to the Sacred College by leading 2 pilgrimages; one to Lourdes on May 30, and one to Rome in October. Possibly you would like to take in the former. I suppose it will occupy about 8 days.

Ever yrs.,

T.Rs.D.B

Note Father Byles' signature line to his brother.

T =Thomas

Rs =Roussel

D=Davids

B=Byles

Chapter 8

Father Byles loved parish life, and teaching the Boy Scouts boxing made it all the more exciting. He had found that teaching boxing gave him a chance for exercise and helped the boys earn their merit badge.

One day in early April, Father Byles sat down at his desk to go through the day's mail. He opened an envelope from the White Star Line offices. He was interrupted by a knock at the door. He called to his housekeeper, "Miss Fields, would you mind opening the door?"

A young English Boy Scout, circa. 1911.

A couple of moments later, Miss Fields announced, "Father, you have received a telegram – I believe it is from your brother William."

Quickly scanning the message, the priest's eyebrows raised in surprise. "Miss Field!" Father Byles exclaimed. You won't believe the news I've just received! My ticket has been switched, and I'm now leaving on the RMS *Titanic* on Easter Wednesday. I'll need to write William and let him know that the ticket has been changed."

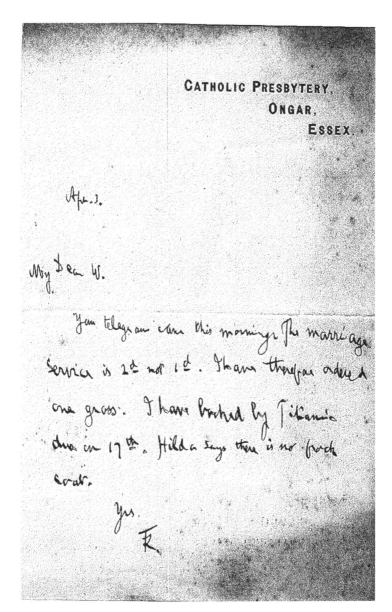

Copy of Father Byles' letter to William, dated April 3,
letting his brother know of his planned passage on the
Titanic, courtesy Joan Byles Barry.

It reads, "My dear W. Your telegram arrived this
morning. The marriage service is the 2nd not the 1st...I
have booked by Titanic due on 17th...Yrs. T.R."

On Easter Monday, Father Watson arrived and soon, the two men were seated at the table, eating a small supper prepared by Miss Field.

"This will be quite the journey, Thomas. Are you excited?" Father Watson inquired.

Father Byles took a bite and then answered his friend. "It will surely be a fine holiday. But what I'm really looking forward to is seeing my brother again."

"Have you ever considered settling down in America, Thomas? It would be such an easier life for you. You would be able to live near your Catholic family and not in this poverty."

Father Byles with several of his parishioners. By all accounts, the priest loved his vocation.

Father Byles smiled. "It would certainly be attractive, but I have no purpose to desert my people. There are several cases in my parish that cause me anxiety. Even leaving them for a few weeks is a concern. I have arranged for my replacement to be in touch with them while I am away."

"You know, this is the season for icebergs," Father Watson warned. "No doubt the *Titanic* is a grand vessel, but do you feel entirely safe crossing the North Atlantic at this time of year?"

Father Byles shook his head. "In every season we must trust ourselves to Providence. Wherever we are, we are in God's hands."

After another hour of visiting Father Watson prepared to take his leave. "I suppose I should be going. Have a good trip, Thomas."

"I'll walk out with you," said Father Byles. "I have to go visit the Nelson family, as I do each Monday evening."

The two walked on for a short distance to the house of a very poor family, and then parted ways. Giving Thomas a hearty handshake, Father Watson said, "I hope you'll come back again," and then walked off into the dark night.

Traditionally, the week after Easter has always been called Easter Week. These weekdays are called Easter Monday, Easter Tuesday, etc. They continue the Easter feast for a full octave.

Chapter 9

Two days later, on Easter Wednesday, April 10, 1912, Father Byles boarded the train at the Epping-Ongar station.

He arrived at the Liverpool Street Station; and then proceeded to the Waterloo Station, and joined the Boat Train for Southampton. At the White Star Line terminal to gain access

Epping-Ongar Station, Circa 1912.

to *Titanic*, Father Byles waited in line for about ten minutes, before finally reaching the front desk.

"Good morning Father, how are you?" the clerk asked.

"I'm doing quite well, my good man. Thank you for asking," Father Byles said with a smile.

Epping-Ongar Station railroad tracks. This is the station from which Father Byles departed.

"May I see your ticket? I'm sure you'd like to get on board as soon as possible."

"Certainly," Father Byles responded. Reaching into his pocket, he pulled out his ticket and handed it to the clerk.

Inspecting the ticket and comparing it to his records, the clerk read out loud. "Ticket #244310, Reverend Thomas Byles, second-class passenger? Is that correct?"

"Yes indeed."

Passengers prepare to depart.

"Very good. You can proceed on to C-Deck, please board through the aft gangway. Enjoy your voyage, Father Byles!"

"Thank you very much!" the kindly priest said, waving at the young man.

As he walked toward the gangway, Father Byles craned his neck to take in the sheer size of *Titanic*. The mighty ship loomed above the water line. Its great length stretched along the pier for a distance nearly the length of three rugby fields.

Father Byles' ticket number for passage on Titanic was Ticket #244310.

Remembering back to his conversation with Tommy, Father Byles realized that in its vast enormity, the ship really did seem unsinkable.

The Royal Mail Steamer *Titanic*.
Titanic was 882 feet 9 inches long and 104 feet high (from the keel to the top of the bridge).

Near the gangway entrance a steward greeted him and directed him to the purser's office. There, he received his room number and had a steward assigned to him.

After Father Byles arrived at his berth and put away his luggage, he walked around the ship, exploring the many sights.

As he strolled the promenade deck, a shrill whistle blew, indicating departure. Together with hundreds of other passengers Father Byles pressed against the ship's dock side railing and waved good-bye to Southampton.

As was the custom, a torrent of fresh white flowers, which had been provided to them by the White Star Line, fell from the hands of the passengers and into the water, leaving a veil-like covering on the wake.

Planned route of *Titanic* from Southampton to New York. The star marks the spot where *Titanic* sank.

Chapter 10

Captain Edward J. Smith was one of the most renowned captains of his time. *Titanic* was to be his final voyage before retiring.

Later the same day, Father Byles sought out Captain Edward Smith, to make arrangements for offering Mass while on board the *Titanic*. Father found Captain Smith on the bridge, introduced himself and made his request.

"Certainly, Father," Captain Smith answered cordially. "I'll be leading a Church of England service for First Class passengers and Reginald Barker will be leading a service for second class. However I'm sure a Mass would be appreciated by the Catholics on board second class. The library on C Deck can be reserved for this purpose. I'll leave you to make the arrangements."

During the brief journey to Cherbourg, Father Byles wrote a letter to his housekeeper:

"Dear Miss Field,
On board ship one has little to do to fill up time so I start to write a letter to you which will be posted at Queenstown tomorrow morning. Everything so far has gone very well, except that I have somehow managed to lose my

This is the first page of Father Byles' letter to Miss Fields. The letter was posted by Fr. Byles at Queenstown. Written on White Star Line stationary, the letter has yellowed with age. Courtesy of Joan Byles Barry.

umbrella. I first missed it getting out of the train at Southampton, but am inclined to think that I left it at Liverpool Street. We arrived at Southampton in the boat train at 11:30 and started at 12 o'clock very punctually. At

one we had lunch. We were then still in Southampton
Water, but when we came out of lunch we were between
Portsmouth and the Isle of Wight.

Before coming out of supper we had stopped at
Cherbourg, and the tender was just coming alongside with
passengers. The tender is a good sized boat of 1260 tons,
but by the side of Titanic she looks as though with a good
crane we could lift her out of the water and lay her on the
deck without feeling any inconvenience. The decks are like
this

1. Top deck for promenading
2. Second deck (1st class only) for promenading
   Promenade
3. Deck b. 2nd class smoking room, promenading on
   both sides Deck
4. –C Library, closed in promenade on both sides
   Upper Deck
5. –D Dining Saloon and some cabins Saloon Deck
6. –E Cabins – Swimming Bath – Turkish Bath Main
   Deck
7. –F Cabins Middle Deck
8. –G Cabins Lower Deck

That makes 8 decks above the water line. When you look
down at the water from the top deck it is like looking from
the roof of a very high building. At the time of writing
(7.45) we are still stopping at Cherbourg.

The English Channel was decidedly rough to look at, but
we felt it no more in the roughest part than when we were

in Southampton Water. I do not much like the throbbing of the screws, but that is the only motion we feel. I have found two other priests among the 2nd class passengers – one a Benedictine from Bavaria, and one a secular from Lithuania. I shall not be able to say

Titanic's giant propellers

Mass to-morrow morning, as we shall be just arriving at Queenstown and there will consequently be some confusion, but after that there will be no difficulty about it. This letter will be posted in Queenstown tomorrow morning. Of course I must put it in the letter box before we arrive there, so I shall not be able to acknowledge the receipt of any letter that may come there for me. I trust Ben went back home alright on Monday morning. I will write as soon as I get to New York & you should probably have my letter between the 24th and the 29th.

Believe me
Yours Truly
T.R.D. Byles

The following day, Father Byles had a quick breakfast and then told Catholic passengers that he was available for Confession. This resulted in most of the day being spent celebrating the Sacrament of Penance. When night came, Father Byles took his dinner in the second

Second class dining room on the RMS *Olympic*, *Titanic*'s sister ship. The second class dining room of *Titanic* was virtually identical to *Olympic*.

class dining room. Afterwards he retired.

On the morning of April 14th, Father Byles rose early to prepare for Mass. He brought the sacred vessels to the sycamore-paneled library and carefully unpacked the portable altar stone he had brought on board for just this purpose. It was the octave of Easter, also known as "Thomas Sunday" because the gospel reading told the story of the post-resurrection encounter between Jesus and Thomas the Apostle. By the time Mass started, the library was filled with worshippers.

Father Byles recited the opening prayer in Latin, "Grant, we beseech Thee, O almighty God, that we who have completed the observance of the paschal festival, may keep it, by Thy bounty, in our life and behavior. Through our Lord."

The Liturgy of the Word continued and Father Byles read the Epistle 1 John 5:4-10 and the Gospel According to Saint John 20:19-31. After the Gospel reading about his patron, "doubting" Thomas, Father Byles began his homily in English with great fervor and energy.

"My dear people, you are traveling across the sea on a wonderful ocean liner to a wonderful new land. Such a journey is rich with opportunity and hope; but there is also the possibility of danger, of spiritual shipwreck.

On a sea voyage, your physical life is buoyed up by the use of a lifebelt. But it is also necessary to have a spiritual lifebelt, to guard against spiritual shipwreck.

A lifejacket also known as a lifebelt circa 1912. This is the type of lifejacket that Father Byles would have worn onboard *Titanic*.

That lifebelt takes the shape of prayer and the sacraments. When one is in danger of spiritual shipwreck, and by this I mean temptation, he must rely on being buoyed by the graces provided through the reception of the Sacraments and a fervent prayer life..."

Chapter 11

That night, April 14, 1912, Father Byles felt restless. Dressed in his long cassock and also wearing an overcoat due to the freezing temperature, he took his Breviary onto the deck. Silently murmuring Compline, Father Byles walked around the deck. He noticed again how very cold it was.

Suddenly, there was a sharp jolt, the ship rocked,

Iceberg in mid-Atlantic, photographed late 1912. Many believe that this may be the iceberg that *Titanic* struck, both from its location and from red paint on its side.

and Father Byles grabbed onto the railing to prevent himself from falling.

When he caught his footing, Father Byles looked up and saw chards of ice on the deck of the great ship. The ship's engines had stopped, and the vessel was not moving.

Father Byles hurried down to the passengers in steerage, for whom he had offered a second Mass that morning. He was confronted by a scene of frightened, confused passengers frantically speaking to one another in a cacophony of languages. The impact had been felt more keenly in these lower regions of the ship, awaking sleeping passengers and even throwing some of them from their beds.

Raising his hands, Father Byles spoke firmly, "Be calm, my good people!" All eyes looked toward him, and he then took the opportunity to offer general absolution and blessings.

The noise of escaping steam from the boilers grew louder and louder, pushing the initial sense of uneasiness toward outright panic. Father Byles again raised his hands and called out again, "My friends! Let us pray!" Those around him were soothed by his calm assurance and readily followed him in the prayers of the rosary.

The Rosary is a meditative prayer using prayer beads, an ancient, historic practice. The prayer consists of the Creed, the Our Father (or Pater Noster), the Glory Be, and a series of Hail Marys. The Hail Mary prayer recalls Gabriel's greeting to Mary from the Gospel of Luke, "Hail, Full of Grace, the Lord is with thee." The response is from Elizabeth's greeting to Mary, "Blessed are you among women."

Chapter 12

After praying the Rosary, Father Byles led a group of third class passengers up several stairways to the top deck. A blast of chilling air shocked them. The good priest shivered, yet remained stalwart as he motioned for the others who were hesitant to come onto deck.

The stewards continued to try to lighten the chilling mood. The band was even playing Ragtime tunes. However, the white faces and whispers of the crew made many fearfully question why they had all been summoned on deck. But, many were jolted into reality as officers and sailors called out "Lower the lifeboats! Women and children first!"

Hearing this order, Father Byles turned and looked for women or children nearby. When he saw a young woman with a baby in her arms and a toddler by her side, he hurried over to her.

"Come along, my dear. Let's get you and your little ones into this boat, shall we?" Father Byles asked her quietly.

The woman looked around at the grand ship and then at the slight lifeboat. She clutched her baby daughter tighter and pulled the toddler closer to her.

"I've heard that there isn't anything to these rumors, but now the officers are saying to get into the boats! This ship isn't really sinking, is it Father?" she asked in a frightened voice.

THE SAD PARTING—THE LAST "GOOD-BYS." PLACING WOMEN IN THE LIFEBOATS

Although some realized very quickly how fatal the crash had been, many were reluctant to leave the apparent safety of the *Titanic* for a cold night in a lifeboat. As the lifeboats were filled, many families were separated, praying that they would see each other again. Most of them never did.

Father Byles smiled at her, and picked up the little boy beside her, who had begun to whimper. "My good lady, as a precaution, all women and children are being loaded into the lifeboats. These officers know what they are doing-please get in, if not for your sake, then for your children's."

The young woman nodded and moved toward a lifeboat. Helping her up over the high bulwark, Father Byles then handed her the toddler he was carrying.

As the boat began to leave the ship, Father Byles raised his hands in blessing. Calling upon heaven, the priest begged for grace to be extended to those in the lifeboat, many of whom he knew may never see their loved ones again.

Chapter 13

After just a half hour on deck, the elements had started to take their toll on everyone. Those in the lifeboats were almost as frightened as those left onboard, having departed for the most part with no food, water, or lights. Father Byles, having helped countless souls, realized that he had failed to put on his gloves before coming on deck. His freezing fingers had traced the Sign of the Cross on every head that he had helped into a lifeboat.

An artist's representation of lifeboats leaving the *Titanic*. 36 lifeboats were planned in Thomas Andrews' original design. He was overruled by Bruce Ismay, and *Titanic* set sail with only 20 lifeboats. It would prove to be a catastrophic error.

Someone touched his shoulder. "Father, there's a seat in this lifeboat. Please get in!" a sailor begged.

"No, my friend. All women and children must be away

before I go," Father Byles replied, recognizing the young sailor as one of the men who had attended the second cabin Mass that morning.

A few minutes later, the sailor begged him again. "Please Father! Another seat is empty. Get in!"

With a small smile, Father Byles gently shook his head and moved on to the next lifeboat.

Last known photograph of Father Thomas Byles

The sailor sighed in intense frustration and disappointment. "I don't understand you priests! Don't you value your life? I've offered a seat in the lifeboats twice to you, and I've offered the same seat to that foreign priest over there. He wouldn't take it either. I'm ashamed to admit it, but if I were you, I'd jump at a chance for survival."

Father Byles turned and his eyes met those of Father Josef Peruschwitz, a Bavarian priest. He had met Father Peruschwitz earlier in the trip and had admired him very much. Now, they were sharing in their priestly duties.

Turning back toward the distressed sailor, the kindly priest patted him on the shoulder. "It is not because I do not value my life. It is because I must help others learn to value theirs."

Turning from the sailor, Father Byles walked over to a group of young ladies.
"Let's get you ladies into a lifeboat, shall we?" Father Byles asked them.

The eldest of the girls looked around fearfully. "I don't know what to do, Father! The ship looks so much safer than those little boats."

One of *Titanic's* collapsible lifeboats. It was photographed by a passenger onboard the *Carpathia*, in the morning of April 15, 1912.

"My dear Miss Mocklare, this ship is sinking. It will be at the bottom of the ocean in a couple of hours. It is anything but safe. I promise you that those in the lifeboats will take good care of you and ensure that, to the best of their ability, no harm comes to you."

Swallowing hard, Miss Mocklare nodded and moved toward the lifeboats. The girls behind her followed hesitantly. Father Byles, smiling and whispering prayers the whole time, helped them into the boats.

As he turned from helping more women and children into the boats, the priest grasped with a death-like hold onto the ship's rail. The deck was now tilting so far forward that it was a miracle that so few people had tumbled into the icy Atlantic waters. But after being on deck for over three hours, the cold air had already started to take its toll. Father Byles' fingers could scarcely ball into a fist because they were so numb.

Father Byles paused for a moment and took in the chaotic scene in front of him. It all seemed like one awful nightmare. Just yesterday, the ship had towered above the icy waters, and now she inched nearer and nearer to those calm yet deadly depths. He remembered the words of Tommy back home.

"I've heard that not even God could sink that ship."

How wrong those rumors had been! But how could anyone have imagined that the *Titanic* would really hit the ocean floor? Father Byles strived to regain his confidence and courage.

As Father Byles looked across the deck at the remaining few women and children, his heart was broken anew as he saw a group of three bell boys grouped together. These

lads, employed on the ship, stood stalwartly directing the ladies toward the boats and never making one move toward any themselves.
Though their faces were pale from the cold, they chatted good-naturedly.

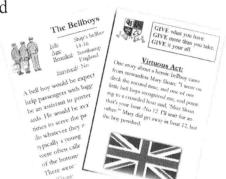

Father Byles walked over to them and quietly said, "You lads are a shining example of courage in the midst of all this chaos and fear. I'm privileged to know you."

One of the young men grinned at him. "Thanks, Father. Good to meet you too. Pray for us tonight, will you? We're all going to need it…" his voice trailed off as tears shimmered in his courageous brown eyes.

Bell boys employed on Titanic were expected to carry luggage for passengers and also served as aides to porters. They were nicknamed "buttons" because of the buttons on their uniforms.
None survived the sinking.
The image used on this page is from the Titanic Heroes card set, available at www.TitanicHeroes.com.

Father Byles' eyes also filled and he raised his right hand in blessing. Immediately, all three boys fell to their knees. And as Father Byles whispered the familiar Latin words, he prayed for their continued strength.

Chapter 14

Artist's representation of the *Titanic* sinking

Eventually, the last lifeboat was cast off from the ship. An eerie silence fell over the deck, as all those left onboard realized that they were watching their last hope for survival depart. Seeing that his task of helping the women and children into boats had been fulfilled, Father Byles then turned to the spiritual needs of those left on deck. The priest began to look for something that would make him stand higher, anything that would enable him to see those remaining on the once great *Titanic*.

A tall coil of rope was lying on one side of the tilting deck. Father Byles walked toward it, slowly making his way through the throngs of people, mostly men, still onboard. He climbed slowly on top of the rope- the priest, like everyone else onboard the sinking ship, had slackened his pace considerably because of the freezing air that bit viciously at his back, neck, face, and hands.

Raising his voice and shouting as loud as he could, Father Byles cried, "Let us pray!"

A sketch of Father Byles' last minutes. This drawing was sketched by a survivor onboard the *Carpathia*. It was given to William Byles after the disaster. William did not believe the face was an accurate likeness of his brother so he cut out Fr. Byles' face from an old photo and pasted it onto the drawing. He then made a copy for the family. This is a picture of that copy. The original burned in a fire on Wall Street, while the copy survived with only a tear on the right-hand side.

Hundreds of eyes turned toward the priest. Without speaking, groups of men began to move near him. They removed their hats and bowed their heads in prayer. Father Byles shouted the words of general absolution as loud as he possibly could, and as sounds began to grow louder, Father Byles began to pray the Rosary.

Hundreds of voices mixed with his. Catholic, Protestants, and Jews alike all began to pray, turning to God in their final hour.

"Holy Mary, Mother of God, pray for us sinners, now and at the hour of our death! Amen!"

A commemorative card celebrating the valiant actions of the *Titanic* musicians. It was produced a couple months after the disaster.

Their voices mixed with the sounds of music. The brave musicians onboard the *Titanic* gave what they had. They continued to play until they could give no more. As the icy water inched closer and closer, the orchestra played "Nearer My God to Thee."

With sounds soaring toward Heaven, the ship's stern began to rise fully into the air. Those still left onboard the ship, including Father Byles, began to slide down the deck, colliding with anything in their uncontrollable path.

As the *Titanic* sank lower into the water, there was a deafening crash that even those in the lifeboats heard. The ship split into two huge pieces, and the electric lights onboard the ship went out, plunging those in the lifeboats into darkness.

The *Titanic* was now almost perpendicular in the water, her stern completely in the air. She remained there for the space of about half a minute, then slowly and quietly, the great liner sank below the surface of the water.

Screams began to echo across the ocean. That utterly calm, silent, beautiful night had become one of unimaginable terror and sorrow. Those in the lifeboats heard the moans of dying souls, some freezing in the water and some drowning. Father Thomas Byles was among them.

The sounds continued for what seemed like hours to the desolate and sorrowful people on board the lifeboats until finally, everything was gravely silent.
The great ocean liner that had been an "unsinkable" dream for so many, now became a tomb for hundreds of souls.

Epilogue

The RMS *Carpathia* arrived at 4:00 AM, on April 15,

Survivors onboard the RMS *Carpathia*.

1912. Its Captain, Arthur Rostron, had plowed through dangerous ice fields to reach the last known coordinates of the *Titanic*. In a stroke of irony, the passengers of the White Star Line's flagship, the great *Titanic*, were now being rescued by the tiny *Carpathia*, a ship in the Cunard Line – the White Star Line's main rival.

By 9:00 AM, Second Officer Charles Lightoller became the last survivor of *Titanic* to board the *Carpathia*. While the passengers of the *Carpathia* did all that they could to aid the *Titanic*'s survivors, the remaining trip to New York was full of grief, worry, and heartache.

When news of the *Titanic*'s sinking reached New York, it made international headlines. Over 1500 passengers, mostly men, were lost at sea. The temperature was reported to be 28 degrees Fahrenheit that night. Father Thomas Byles was not among the survivors, and his body was never recovered.

A picture of some of those anxiously awaiting news of their relatives, friends, or benefactors. Hundreds of those waiting would never see their loved ones again. William Byles would have been among them.

When news of the tragedy reached William Byles, he and Katherine went ahead with their scheduled wedding, but it was a simple and somber affair. Immediately following the ceremony, they attended a memorial Mass for their beloved Roussel (Thomas).

William and Katherine traveled to Bernardsville, New Jersey, to learn more about the sinking. They visited survivors and the White Star Line Offices to investigate into the accident. It was then that William wrote the following letter to his mother-in-law.

April 21, 1912

My dear Mamma,

Here we are at Bernardsville. We went to St. Vincent's Hospital, when we met first some young boys and afterwards some girls who had been on the Titanic. There were a large number of the survivors there, being fitted out with clothes used for relief. Whilst we were there the Cardinal came in and we had the privilege of a few minutes with him in the corridor.

He spoke very nicely of Roussel and of all the good he must have done on board. The survivors told us they saw him on deck every day, so that evidently Roussel was at least fairly well. On Sunday afternoon Roussel had Rosary and prayers and preached a sermon on the new life they were to enter into in America and the dangers to their Faith they had to guard against-his last sermon.

After the accident Roussel appeared on deck in full clothes and moved about among the crowd from group to group giving absolution (without confessions) and starting all the Catholics on the Rosary. One girl said the sailors wanted to put him into a lifeboat, but he refused, and went on with his work. The passengers were all together on the higher decks – First, Second and Third all mixed up, so all participated in his ministrations.

Can you see all those poor people saying the Rosary, and Our Lady at the other end of the Rosary pulling some of them into lifeboats, and others to hear the happy command, "Enter thou into the joy of the Lord."?

From St. Vincent's we went to the Chelsea Hotel, where we met Mr. & Mrs. Bean, who had only been married a month, and were both saved together. They knew little, but they gave us the address of Roussel's cabin companion. If he has been saved, we may hear more from him. Father Clifford will offer a public Mass on Wednesday.

Goodbye, Mamma, and many, many thanks for giving me Katherine. She shall always be my greatest treasure – a pearl of great price. Pray for us every day that we may join Roussel and May [William's sister-in-law], where they are all now together.

Yours affectionately,

William

Father Thomas Byles died as he had lived, giving whatever he had, even his life. He gave his all, whether that was his priestly duties or his place in the lifeboat. Throughout his life, but also through his death, he served as a model of fortitude, perseverance, and incredible charity.

Rev. J Cooreman, SJ, summed up Father Byles' life in these words when he wrote a condolence letter to William in 1912, "He died a Martyr of charity, performing the most perfect act of love of God and of his neighbor."

100 years later...
Saint Helen's

Left: A commemorative window was installed at St. Helen's after the sinking. In the middle triptych, Jesus as the Good Shepherd is depicted.
On the right is St. Thomas Aquinas.
On the left is St. Patrick.

Below: The dedication of the window to Father Byles.

Pray for the Rev Thomas Byles for 8 years Rector of this mission whose heroic death in the disaster to S.S Titanic April 15 1912 earnestly devoting his last moments to the religious consolation of his fellow passengers this window commemorates

100 years later…
Epping Ongar Railway

Above: Epping Ongar Railway today.
Below: The dedication of a plaque to Father Byles in 2012.
Courtesy Ongar Historical Society.

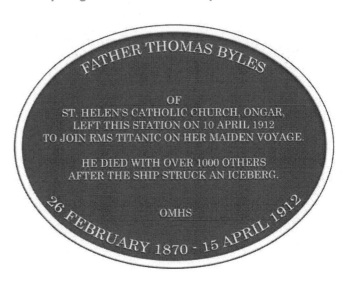

FATHER THOMAS BYLES

OF
ST. HELEN'S CATHOLIC CHURCH, ONGAR,
LEFT THIS STATION ON 10 APRIL 1912
TO JOIN RMS TITANIC ON HER MAIDEN VOYAGE.

HE DIED WITH OVER 1000 OTHERS
AFTER THE SHIP STRUCK AN ICEBERG.

OMHS

26 FEBRUARY 1870 - 15 APRIL 1912

100 years later...
The Coast Guard's
International Ice Patrol

The sinking of the RMS *Titanic* shocked the world. But

shortly afterward, an international effort culminated in the creation of the International Ice Patrol whose mission is to monitor the iceberg danger near the Grand

Banks of Newfoundland. Since 1913 the United States Coast Guard has been tasked with the management and operation of the patrol.

Since about 1923, the Coast Guard has honored those who lost their lives on the

RMS *Titanic* with an annual wreath drop over the site of the sinking.

In 2012, the one hundredth anniversary of the sinking, Father Thomas Byles was specifically honored in the wreath drop by Cady Crosby, the author of this book.

Father Byles' wreath is blessed by Archbishop Kevin Boland of the Apostleship of the Sea.

Father Byles' wreath is dropped on April 15th, 2012 over the site of the sinking. This location is a graveyard to many people and should remain untouched.

Historical Notes

In the summer of 2011, I was asked a question by my mother, and that question was, "Do you know if there were any priests onboard the *Titanic*?" We had just been discussing the fact that the hundredth anniversary of *Titanic's* demise was rapidly approaching, and as a devout Roman Catholic family, the question of spiritual life onboard entered our minds. I stepped over to the computer and it took me barely a minute to find the answer – namely, that there were three Catholic priests onboard and all three died administering their priestly blessing. Of all three priests, I could find the most information about Fr. Thomas Byles.

After reading about Father Byles' life and being inspired by this heroic man of God, I embarked on a quest. That quest was to write, edit, and eventually publish in some way the book you now hold in your hands. Doing this proved difficult but rewarding, as most things worth doing are. However, because of the lack of information about Father Byles, I (as the author) had to make a couple judgment calls regarding the stories I told and the actions that I related. This means that this book fits into a genre called "historical fiction." Historical fiction is a story based on real facts and real people, with some additional story lines from the author's research.

This book fits that description very well. Father Byles' early life is not well documented and scenes such as Roussel conversing with Lawrence and his mother, Roussel at church…these scenes are from my imagination. They are based upon what I believe the Byles parents, being the God-fearing people that they were, would have taught their children.

Father Byles did teach boys of his parish boxing and was an eager proponent of Scouting. However, there is no solid proof that a St. Helen's Boy Scout troop really did exist-though the possibility is very real.

The relationship between Monsignor Watson and Father Byles has been well-documented, and Monsignor Watson himself spoke of it often in his memoirs. The text of the conversations are from my imagination however – their idea first stemmed from historical incidents. The quote from Msgr. Watson is taken from an article written July 1912 by Monsignor Edward Watson. The article can be viewed at www.FatherByles.com.

Father Byles did ask Captain Smith to offer Mass, offered Mass on Sunday (and all other days excepting that mentioned in the letter), and really did preach a homily on the need for a spiritual lifebelt in case of spiritual shipwreck.

For further study, I would highly recommend Father Scott Archer's website www.FatherByles.com.

Citations

All pictures of Father Thomas Byles and family are used with permission from Mrs. Joan Byles Barry the grandniece of Father Byles. Text of the letters from Father Byles to various individuals is also used with permission from Mrs. Joan Byles Barry.

Pictures of the Epping-Ongar Train Station are used with permission from the Epping-Ongar Train Station, which is still operating in England.

All illustrations, excepting those aforementioned, are public domain images and are from Wikimedia Commons.

Monsignor Edward Watson, *Reminiscences*, July 1912. The Edmundian. Retrieved from www.FatherByles.com, July 19, 2012.

The quote on page 22 is from the Ongar Millennium History Society and used with permission from Mr. John Winslow.

"Matthew 25:40." *The Holy Bible: New King James Version*. N.p.: Tyndale, 1982.

The New American Bible. Northport, NY: Costello Pub., 1988.

Acknowledgements

The author would like to acknowledge:

Mrs. Joan Byles Barry, USA. Mrs. Byles Barry, thank you so much for all you contributed to this project. I am privileged to have been able to correspond with you. Thank you also for permission to use Byles family pictures. They add a historical element that otherwise would be lost. Thank you for your encouragement, patience, and willingness to help a young author.

Father Scott Archer, USA. Father Archer, before I found your site, I had never heard of Father Byles. Prior to the centennial of the sinking in 2012, there was almost nothing on the internet regarding Father Byles other than your site. But now, many more know the story of this heroic priest and many, like me, have unearthed his story by finding your website. Thank you for keeping Fr. Byles' legacy alive!

Snowy Evans, *Scouting in Ongar*, UK. Thank you for being willing to send me your book about scouting- it gave me a way to make the story about the St. Helen's Boy Scout troop much more plausible.

John Winslow, Ongar Millennium Historical Society, UK. Thank you for your willingness to contribute to this project and encouraging me.

Simon Hanney, Epping-Ongar Train Station, UK. Thank you so much for allowing me to use the pictures of the Epping-Ongar Train Station. I appreciate your generosity and willingness to help with this project. I hope someday to take you up on the offer to come to the station!

Mrs. Katherine Eames, USA. Mrs. Eames, thank you for encouraging me by saying you thought my book was good but "it could be better." Thanks for urging me to "GIVE it my all" and make the book what it is today. You're a phenomenal example of a godly woman and I'm privileged to know you!

Mrs. Julia Fogassy, USA. Mrs. Fogassy, I am so indebted to you for all that you have done with and for me on this project. This book wouldn't be even close to what it now is without your help. Thank you for being an amazing example of the 3G principles – I am honored and grateful for your willingness to pour into my life. Your tireless efforts to help and inspire me are amazing-thank you so much.

My family. Thank you all for being with me on this journey. Mommy, thanks for your endless work with me on the ins and outs of the book. Daddy, Benjamin, Sarah, Lucy, Mary, and Terinda, thanks for setting things aside so I could work on this. Love you all!

The valiant men and women onboard the RMS *Titanic* 100 years ago. Thank you for being willing to make the ultimate sacrifice when it was required of you. Your stories and examples have lived on for 100 years and will live on as a shining example to every generation.

A lifeboat full of *Titanic* survivors is lifted aboard the *Carpathia*, on the morning of April 15, 1912.

About the Author

Cady Crosby is fifteen years old, homeschooled, and in ninth grade. She lives with her parents, Robert and Tena Crosby, and her five siblings in Washington State. The story of Father Thomas Byles inspired Cady and her brother Benjamin to create Titanic Heroes© www.TitanicHeroes.com.

Titanic Heroes© exists to teach and inspire people to live the 3G Principles by sharing stories of historical heroism.

Father Byles' story lives on in their one hour living history presentation which is part-drama, part-motivational message and is just one aspect of what this inspiring team has to offer.

Cady blogs at www.flameoffaith.blogspot.com and would welcome any visits to the site.

Titanic Heroes©
www.TitanicHeroes.com

Made in the USA
Charleston, SC
17 May 2013